AMERICA'S CHAMPION SWIMMER

· · · · · · · · ·

Gertrude Ederle

WRITTEN BY

David A. Adler

ILLUSTRATED BY

Terry Widener

Gulliver Books

Harcourt, Inc.

SAN DIEGO   NEW YORK   LONDON

Gulliver Books is a registered trademark of Harcourt, Inc.

Library of Congress Cataloging-in-Publication Data
Adler, David A.
America's champion swimmer: Gertrude Ederle/David A. Adler;
illustrated by Terry Widener.
p.   cm.
"Gulliver Books."
Summary: Describes the life and accomplishments of Gertrude Ederle,
the first woman to swim the English Channel and a figure in the early
women's rights movement.
1. Ederle, Gertrude, 1906–   —Juvenile literature.   2. Swimmers—
United States—Biography—Juvenile literature.   3. Women swimmers—
United States—Biography—Juvenile literature.   [1. Ederle, Gertrude,
1906–   .   2. Swimmers.   3. Women—Biography.]
I. Widener, Terry, ill.   II. Title.
GV838.E34A35   2000
797.2'1' 092—dc21
[B]   98-54954
ISBN 0-15-201969-3

First edition
F E D C B A

The illustrations in this book were done in Golden acrylics on
Strathmore Bristol board.
The display type was set in Bernhard Gothic and Stuyvesant.
The text type was set in Fournier.
Color separations by Bright Arts Ltd., Hong Kong
Printed and bound by Phoenix Color Corp., Rockaway, New Jersey
This book was printed on totally chlorine-free Nymolla Matte Art paper.
Production supervision by Stanley Redfern
Designed by Michael Farmer

For Mom, a real champion

—D. A. A.

For Kate, Kellee, and girls everywhere—
dream big and believe in yourself

—T. W.

In 1906 women were kept out of many clubs and restaurants. In most states they were not allowed to vote. Many people felt a woman's place was in the home.

But Gertrude Ederle's place was in the water.

Gertrude Ederle was born on October 23, 1906. She was the third of six children and was raised in New York City, where she lived in an apartment next to her father's butcher shop. Her family called her Gertie. Most everyone else called her Trudy.

Trudy spent her early years playing on the sidewalks of New York. It wasn't until she was seven that she had her first adventure in the water. While visiting her grandmother in Germany, Trudy fell into a pond and nearly drowned.

After that near disaster, Trudy's father was determined to teach her to swim. For her first lesson, he tied one end of a rope to Trudy's waist and held on to the other end. He put Trudy into a river and told her to paddle like a dog.

Trudy mastered the dog paddle. She joined her older sister Margaret and the other children in the water and copied their strokes. Soon Trudy swam better than any of them.

From that summer on, it was hard to keep Trudy out of the water. She *loved*
to swim. At the age of thirteen she became a member of the New York
Women's Swimming Association and took lessons there.

At fifteen Trudy won her first big race.

The next year, she attempted to be the first woman to swim the more than seventeen miles from lower Manhattan to Sandy Hook, New Jersey. When Trudy slowed down, her sister Margaret yelled, "Get going, lazybones!" And Trudy did. She finished in just over seven hours. And she beat the men's record.

People were beginning to notice Gertrude Ederle. Newspapers described her as courageous, determined, modest, and poised. They called her the most perfect swimmer. Trudy's mother said she was "just a plain home girl."

In 1924 this "plain home girl" was good enough to make the U.S. Olympic team. Trudy won three medals at the games in Paris. Her team won more points than all the other countries' swimming teams combined.

By 1925 Trudy had set twenty-nine U.S. and world records. She was determined to take on the ultimate challenge: the English Channel. Many had tried
to swim the more-than-twenty-mile-wide body of cold, rough water that
separates England from France. But only five men—and no women—had ever
made it all the way across.

Many people were sure Trudy couldn't do it. A newspaper editorial
declared that Trudy wouldn't make it and that women must admit they would
"remain forever the weaker sex."

It didn't matter to Trudy what people said or wrote. She was going to swim
the Channel.

Early in the morning on August 18, 1925, Trudy stepped into the water at Cape Gris-Nez, France, the starting point for the swim. For almost nine hours she fought the strong current. Then, when Trudy had less than seven miles to go, her trainer thought she had swallowed too much water and pulled her, crying, from the sea.

Trudy did not give up her dream. She found a new trainer, and a year later, on Friday, August 6, 1926, she was ready to try again.

Trudy wore a red bathing cap and a two-piece bathing suit and goggles that she and her sister Margaret had designed. To protect her from the icy cold water, Margaret coated Trudy with lanolin and heavy grease. The greasing took a long time—too long for Trudy. "For heaven's sake," she complained. "Let's get started."

Finally, at a little past seven in the morning, she stepped into the water. "Gee, but it's cold," Trudy said.

Trudy's father, her sister Margaret, her trainer, and a few other swimmers were on board a tugboat named *Alsace*. The boat would accompany Trudy to make sure she didn't get lost in the fog and was safe from jellyfish, sharks, and the Channel's powerful currents. There was a second boat, too, with reporters and photographers on board.

As the *Alsace* bobbed up and down in the choppy water, Margaret wrote in chalk on the side of the boat, "This way, Ole Kid." She drew an arrow that pointed to England.

To entertain Trudy, Margaret and some of the others sang American songs, including "The Star-Spangled Banner" and "East Side, West Side." Trudy said the songs kept her "brain and spirit good."

At first the sea was calm.

Trudy swam so fast that her trainer was afraid she would tire herself out. He ordered her to slow down.

Trudy refused.

At about ten-thirty in the morning, Trudy had her first meal. She floated on her back and ate chicken and drank beef broth. A while later, she ate chocolate and chewed on sugar cubes. Then she swam on.

At about one-thirty in the afternoon, it started to rain. A strong wind stirred the water. For a while, Trudy would swim forward a few feet only to be pulled back twice as far.

By six o'clock the tide was stronger. The waves were twenty feet high. The rough water made the people aboard the *Alsace* and the news boat seasick.

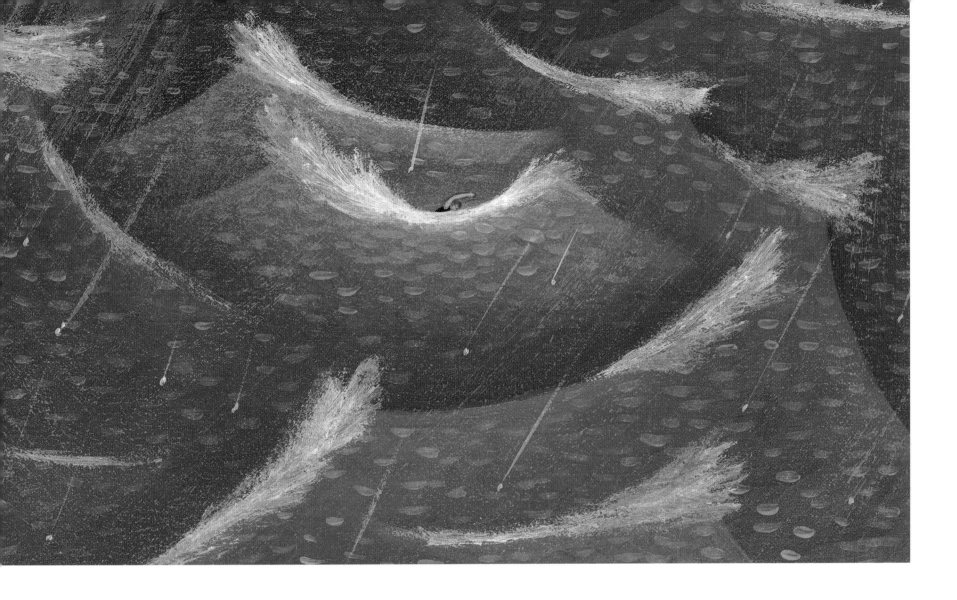

Trudy's trainer was sure she couldn't finish the swim. He told her to give up.

"No, no," Trudy yelled over the sound of the waves. She kept swimming.

In the next few hours, the rain and wind became stronger and the sea rougher. At times the rough water pulled the boats away, out of Trudy's sight. She was scared. It was eerie being out there all alone.

Now Trudy began to have trouble kicking in the water. When the *Alsace* came close again, Trudy said her left leg had become stiff. Her trainer was frightened for her. He yelled, "You must come out."

"What for?" Trudy shouted, and kept swimming.

Trudy continued to fight the tide and the constant stinging spray of water in her face. She knew she would either swim the Channel or drown.

As Trudy neared Kingsdown, on the coast of England, she saw thousands of people gathered to greet her. They lit flares to guide her to shore.

At about nine-forty at night, after more than fourteen hours in the water, Trudy's feet touched land. Hundreds of people, fully dressed, waded into the water to greet her. When she reached the shore, her father hugged Trudy and wrapped her in a warm robe.

"I knew if it could be done, it had to be done, and I did it," Trudy said after she got ashore. "All the women of the world will celebrate."

Trudy swam the Channel in just fourteen hours and thirty-one minutes. She beat the men's record by almost two hours. In newspapers across the world, Trudy's swim was called history making. Reporters declared that the myth that women are the weaker sex was "shattered and shattered forever."

Trudy sailed home aboard the SS *Berengaria*. After six days at sea, the ship entered New York Harbor.

Two airplanes circled and tipped their wings to greet Trudy. People on boats of all kinds rang their bells and tooted their horns to salute her. Foghorns sounded.

Trudy climbed into an open car for a parade up lower Broadway. An estimated two million people, many of them women, stood and cheered. They threw scraps of newspaper, ticker tape, pages torn from telephone books, and rolls of toilet paper.

When her car arrived at the New York city hall, Mayor Jimmy Walker

praised Trudy for her courage, grace, and athletic prowess. "American women," he said, "have ever added to the glory of our nation."

President Calvin Coolidge sent a message that was read at the ceremony. He called Trudy "America's Best Girl." And she was. Gertrude Ederle had become a beacon of strength to girls and women everywhere.

Notes from the author:

While it's twenty-one miles across the Channel, the rough water makes the actual swim much longer. It was estimated Trudy had to swim thirty-five miles to get across.

Trudy's 1925 swim was cut short because of terrible conditions and because her trainer, Jabez Wolffe, touched her in the water. That touch disqualified the swim. Wolffe had tried to swim the Channel more than twenty times but had never succeeded.

For the 1926 swim Trudy's trainer was Thomas W. Burgess, who in 1911, after many failed attempts, was the second man to swim the Channel.

Someone who witnessed Trudy's swim and more than a dozen other attempts commented that in good weather Trudy would have finished at least four hours sooner.

A *London Daily News* editorial declared women "the weaker sex" the very day of Trudy's successful 1926 swim. The next day, the newspaper didn't back down from that statement but explained that "Miss Ederle is evidently a superwoman."

According to New York City Police Inspector Kuehne, many women felt empowered by Trudy's swim. At Trudy's welcome back to New York, he tried to help one very old woman. He was afraid she would get hurt in the crowd. "I guess I can take care of myself," she told him. Inspector Kuehne said later, "That seemed to be the attitude of most of the women."

On August 28, 1926, three weeks after Trudy's swim, another woman, Mrs. Millie Corson, left the coast of France. Two other swimmers, both men, made the attempt with her. Only Millie Corson made it across. Millie Corson was the first mother to swim the Channel. She got across in fifteen hours and thirty-two minutes, not fast enough to beat Trudy's record but faster than any of the previous male swimmers. Two days later, on August 30, 1926, Ernst Vierkoetter, a German, swam the Channel. He did it in just twelve hours and forty-three minutes, setting a new record.

Gertrude Ederle never married. She lost much of her hearing after her swim, perhaps because of the cold Channel water but more likely the result of childhood measles. She fell sometime in the 1940s and was in a cast for more than four years. Doctors were sure Trudy would be confined to a wheelchair, but she was determined to walk again—and she did. Trudy worked as a dress designer and taught deaf children to swim. She was also a member of the President's Council on Youth Fitness.

The sources for much of the information for this book were periodicals of the time, including the *New York Times*, the *New York World*, and the *Literary Digest*, as well as more recent collective biographies.